The purpose of Nurses Christian Fellowship International (NCFI) is to connect Christian nurses around the world, equipping them to live out their faith in professional practice.

NCFI Website: https://ncfi.org/about-ncfi/

CARES II

Reflections for Nurses

Carrie M. Dameron
Editor

Contributors

Carrie M. Dameron
Martha Fernández Moyano
Bulbuli Mollick
Swee Eng Goh
Ishaku Izang
Tove Giske
Steve Fouch
Gladys Altamirano Garrido

a nurses4him.org publication

nurses4him.org
passion, purpose, prayer

CARES II: Reflections for Nurses

2021 English Only Edition

Requests for information should be addressed to:
ncfi.cares@gmail.com

Printed in the United States of America.

ISBN: 978-0-09888360-7-5 English PDF
ISBN: 978-0-09888360-8-2 Bilingual PDF
ISBN: 978-0-09888360-9-9 English Print Book
ISBN: 978-1-7374649-0-7 Bilingual Print Book
nurses4him.org publication

nurses4him.org
passion, purpose, prayer

Greetings from NCFI President

As nurses, we face a diversity of challenges and opportunities at work, it be in bedside nursing, education, leadership, or research. The devotions and reflections collected in CARES II can serve as a motivator and encourager for us to stay close to Jesus and to be reminded of living our everyday lives in the light of serving God in our profession.

Tove Giske, Norway
President, Nurses Christian Fellowship International

Preface

By Carrie M. Dameron

Welcome to **CARES II: Reflections for Nurses!** To properly celebrate this most recent publication, let's review our journey together and how Nurses Christian Fellowship International (NCFI) devotions began. During the NCFI Congress in Santiago Chile, in 2012, I shared with Barbara White (NCFI President from 2008 to 2016) and her husband, John, about my passion to encourage Christian nurses through devotions. They shared how NCFI was looking for a way to encourage and connect with Christian nurses throughout their six different regions across the globe. From that conversation, **NCFI Cares** (**C**aring **A**cross **R**egions with **E**ncouraging **S**cripture) was launched.

In January 2013, I emailed the first devotion to the International Board and the leaders of more than 30 national fellowships. **NCFI Cares** has been and continues to be an amazing pathway to communicate the peace, hope, and strength of Jesus in a consistent, easily accessible way via bimonthly devotions.

Email, Facebook, and blog posts are great venues for a consistent message, yet a printed publication is needed and preferred in some countries. Thus, in anticipation of the 2016 NCFI Congress in Tagaytay Philippines, NCFI leadership requested a printed compilation of **NCFI Cares** devotions. **CARES**: **Reflections for Nurses** devotional book was published.

Since its inception, the **NCFI Cares** devotions had been translated into Spanish and shared with nurses throughout Latin America. So, it made sense to publish **CARES** as a bilingual book with English devotions translated into Spanish. The format is side-by-side with both English/Spanish translations. Subsequent publications included an English-only version and, most recently, a bilingual English/Chinese version also with side-by-side formatting. All three published editions are available as free downloadable PDF's at https://ncfi.org/resources/ncfi-cares-devotionals/

In several regions or countries, each bimonthly devotion is translated into different languages besides Spanish (such as Chinese and Dutch) and shared with non-English speaking nurses. Also, select devotions are sent out to nurses by national fellowships through their newsletters, emails, and blog posts for regional and country members. How far and wide across the globe, each devotion's reach is only known to our Lord. We celebrate each connection with Him!

In January 2018, **NCFI Cares** celebrated its five-year anniversary and 100th emailed devotion. What a milestone! The bimonthly emails are received by more than 300 nurses and midwives, including 52 national fellowship contacts, 23 International Board members, directors, and staff.

In 2019, Martha (my faithful friend, sister in Christ, and writing partner) proposed a second compilation of devotions from **NCFI Cares.** Without her persistent prayer and faithfulness to God, **CARES II** would have stayed just a "great idea". Together we present the second **CARES II**: **Reflections for Nurses/Cuidados II: Reflexiones para enfermeros--**WooHoo! You can find the bilingual edition as a free download at the NCFI website resource page.

The inclusion of international authors makes **CARES II** amazing. The authors made regular contributions throughout the past four years and live in Argentina, Bangladesh, Nigeria, and Singapore, as well as some guest contributions from Chile, Norway, and the United Kingdom. We hope you will be blessed by the cross-cultural encouragement from our international nursing team.

As I reflect on these and other praise-worthy accomplishments of **NCFI Cares**, I look to the future. I am excited to see how the Lord will continue to use devotions to connect nurses across the globe. Now, more than ever, a pertinent Scripture with personal reflections brings the light of Christ to our modern-day heroes, especially during the COVID-19 pandemic.

I request your prayers for **NCFI Cares**, the authors, and the NCFI Prayer and Care Committee. We are here to serve you. We strive to bring the hope and love of God to build both your personal faith and professional work in Christ Jesus for the glory of God.

Keeping in proper devotional format, I encourage you to reflect on the past year or even five years. Write down all the wonders and mighty deeds the Lord has done personally and professionally for you. Like myself, you may find some bumps along the road, unexpected potholes, and ruts that went on way too long; however, I promise you will praise the Lord for his loving hand amidst both wondrous and troubling times.

Psalm 77:11-14 says:
I will remember the deeds of the LORD;
I will certainly remember Your wonders of old.
I will meditate on all Your work,
and on your deeds with thanksgiving.
Your way, O God, is holy.
What god is great like our God?
You are the God who works wonders;
You have made known your might among the peoples.
Amen!

Preface

By Martha Fernández Moyano

This is the second NCFI Cares book, this one entitled **Cares II: Reflections for Nurses.** It has been a great blessing for me to participate in writing the devotionals and providing the Spanish translation.

In 2012, I met Carrie when I joined the Nurses Christian Fellowship International as an International Board Member during the International Congress held in Chile. At that time, I never imagined I would participate in something as important as the NCFI Prayer and Care Committee. A committee that gives spiritual support and care to all nurses working in the six regions of the world that make up the NCFI. Our primary purpose is helping nurses live out the Word of God and express our thanks and requests through prayer directly to Him.

In 2016, the first book, **Cares: Reflections for Nurses,** was introduced at the NCFI Congress in the Philippines. Many colleagues participated in the publication of devotionals that were both inspirational and encouraging.

Since that time, I have contributed to NCFI Cares as an author and as a translator. I translate each devotion into Spanish and email it to 160 Spanish speaking nurses from NCFI member countries of Argentina, Chile, Colombia, Cuba, and Ecuador, as well as nurses in Bolivia, Brazil, Mexico, Paraguay, Peru, Trinidad Tobago, and Uruguay. They are also shared on the Facebook pages of the national fellowships. I have been blessed to know our work is not in vain and brings glory to God. I receive positive responses from so many nurses on how they have been edified while using the devotionals personally and within their local nurses' groups.

It has been a wonderful thing, God allowing me to contribute to both **CARES** books. They are written to support nurses from different countries, languages and cultures through simple yet inspiring devotions.

I have no doubt that **CARES II** will also be a blessing to numerous professional nurses and students who are struggling to bring the values of Christ to nursing in their daily practice.

"Therefore, encourage one another and build one another up, just as you are doing." (1 Thessalonians 5:11).

Jesus Our Role Model

By Tove Giske

[Jesus asks]"What do you want me to do for you?" (Luke 18:41).

As Christian nurses, we have Jesus as our role model and source of strength. I want to share with you how Jesus sees us from His Kingdom perspective. His perspective teaches us how to see and think about people, provide care for patients and their families, and collaborate with our co-workers.

In John 4:1-29, we read about Jesus who met the Samaritan women at the well. Jesus sees the woman and knows who she is; still, He decides to spend time with her. As we read the text, we can sense the gentleness and the intensity of their conversation and how Jesus touched the woman deep within her spirit. She became convinced that she had met the long-awaited Messiah. This makes her a witness for Christ.

In Luke 19:1-10, we read about Zacchaeus up in the tree. Again, Jesus acts beyond the rules and norms, and sees into the heart and longing of this man. He greets Zacchaeus up in the tree and invites Himself to dinner at Zacchaeus' house. This transforms Zacchaeus. Jesus acknowledged this sinner to be a saved son of Abraham. As a result, Zacchaeus' transformed heart is revealed through his actions.

Jesus often asked questions when He taught and met with people. Have you noticed that? He was interested in understanding people, who they are and how they think. Having Jesus as our role model challenges us to consider - Am I interested in understanding people? Do I take the time to stop and listen to the one that needs me?

One of the stories I like the best from the Gospels is the one about the blind beggar outside Jericho. (Luke 18:35-43). Try to imagine the crowd of people and all the noise. In the middle of this, Jesus recognized the one that needs Him. He stops and asks this wonderful question: "What do you want me to do for you?"

Will you join me in following Jesus' example and practice asking this question: "What do you want me to do for you?"

Read: Luke 18:35-43

Reflect: With your next encounter with patients, colleagues, or students ask, "What do you want me to do for you?"

Prayer: Jesus, open my heart and spirit to hear and respond to the needy in my workplace. Amen.

Global Prayer for International Nurses Day

By Carrie M. Dameron

Then they cried out to the LORD in their trouble: He saved them from their distresses. He sent His word and healed them, and saved them from their destruction. (Psalm 107:19-20).

Every year nurses around the world celebrate Nurse's Day during the 2nd week of May. The date coincides with Florence Nightingale's birthday on May 12th. As we celebrate the work of nursing, we can pray for the needs of nurses and patients around the world. A great prayer prompt is the International Council of Nurse (ICN) Strategic Priorities(1):

Universal Health Coverage
Non-communicable Diseases
Primary Health Care
Human Resources for Health
Person Centred Care
Patient Safety
Antimicrobial Resistance
Mental Health
Immunisation
Sustainable Development Goals

Take time during Nurses Day or Week to not only commemorate the founder of modern-day nursing, but to lift-up the health of each human to the Great Physician. Even though we know complete holistic health will not be achieved until Jesus returns to usher the New Kingdom; we can bring the pain and suffering of God's children to His throne room. Knowing He has the power and ability to bring mercy to this present age.

Read: Psalm 107

Reflect: Which of the above strategic priorities are most relevant to your nation/region?

Prayer: We give thanks to You LORD for Your mercy and for Your wonders to the sons of mankind! We offer sacrifices of thanksgiving and tell of Your works with joyful singing. Amen. (Psalm 107:21-22).

Tests from Upon High

By Martha Fernández Moyano

Blessed is a man who perseveres under trial; for once he has been approved, he will receive the crown of life which the Lord has promised to those who love Him. (James 1:12).

My friend listened silently as the doctor gave the diagnosis, treatments, and a long list of explanations. The doctor, noticing my friend's quietness, stopped and asked her, "Why are you not asking questions?" She replied, "I stopped listening when you said that my small son has Diabetes."

A simple sentence, "Your son has Diabetes." is difficult for a mother to hear. As believers we ask the question, "How does God allow these things to happen?" The Word says, "Blessed is the man." But can you be happy for someone who receives this diagnosis? Is it a punishment or a test? It is common that we have a mistaken concept of what is meant by "testing." (James 1:3, 12). And it is common that we have a wrong concept of what means the word "approved."

Abraham had a similar experience, yet more profound. After many years God gave him a son, whom later God asked Abraham to sacrifice. (Genesis 22:9-12). How is it that we are before God a "friend" of ours delights in our suffering? (James 2:23) Often, we have read that God not only proves us, but allows the test. But whom does God prove? God tests those He loves. Those who are His friends. Difficult as it is to understand we know that God is molding us. Since He has given us form, it is possible that it hurts us. Yet, a tear never escapes from God's notice. He is never going to leave us alone in the tests. Instead, He gives us the assurance in His Word we will be approved beyond what we could expect.

The tests that come from upon high extracts qualities of light that God can sow into our heart: obedience, faith, humility, patience, and total dependence. If you have decided to serve the Lord prepare yourself for the test. Say to the Lord, "Here I am." Trusting that in times of adversity you will be able to reach peace.

Read: Genesis 22:9-14

Reflect: What is the first thing you feel in your life when the tests arrive? What attitude do you take before them?

Prayer: Lord, I need you to help me to be watching and praying so that when the test arrives, I can stand firm in front of them and thus glorify You. Amen.

Giving with Joy

By Steve Fouch

God loves a cheerful giver. (2 Corinthians 9:7).

My youngest daughter has had an innate streak of generosity since she was tiny. Anything she got, she wanted to give away to a sibling or a friend. So much so that we sometimes had to suggest that she needed to hang on to some things that she needed for herself. More than once, she offered her food to someone else, and we had to remind her that she needed to eat as well!

For myself, I am so often aware that being generous can entail real sacrifice – of time as well as of money. In that respect, I have often not been a cheerful giver, parting with my gift out of dutiful reluctance rather than joy.

Yet, when I have been spontaneously generous, it has not ended up feeling like a sacrifice. I remember well an old man begging outside of London Bridge station one cold and dreary December morning. I walked past him because I had no change to give, but I did have the means to cross the road, go into a coffee shop and come back with a hot tea and a hot mince pie to warm him. It was a sacrifice of ten minutes on a busy morning and a small sum of money, but it made a difference to him, and it made me happy.

Giving is part of worship, bringing joy to our heavenly Father – Paul makes this clear in 2 Corinthians 9. It is also an act that gives joy and blessing both to the receiver and the giver of the gift. It is not how much we give but why and how we give that matters – does it come from our heart wanting to bless others and rejoice in their joy, or is it out of a sense of duty?

As NCFI Treasurer, one of my duties is to oversee the giving of sponsorships to those coming to the World Congress every four years. While these are only part of the expenses that delegates face, the joy of seeing people able to come and participate in Congress is such a huge blessing to me. It is also a huge blessing to give thanks back to individuals and fellowships who give to the work of NCFI each year.

Generosity in giving is such a source of joy, and one we so easily miss if we see it just as a duty.

Read: 2 Corinthians 9:6-15

Reflect: Ask the Lord to increase your joy as you support the work of NCFI.

Prayer: Father God, true joy comes from blessings others through the blessings we in turn have received from your hand. Amen.

NCFI Value: Integrity

By Carrie M. Dameron

In all things show yourself to be an example of good deeds, with purity in doctrine, dignified, sound in speech which is beyond reproach. (Titus 2:7-8).

In the Old Testament the word "integrity" conveys the meaning of simplicity, or sincerity of heart and intention, truthfulness, and uprightness. [4] An example is found in God's edict to Solomon: "...if you walk before me as your father David walked, in integrity of heart and honesty" (1 Kings 9:4).

In the New Testament there is no exact Greek word for integrity. Instead, translators use "pure of heart" and "sincerity" to imply integrity. We see an example in apostle Paul's instructions to Titus "...in all things show yourself to be an example of good deeds, with purity in doctrine, dignified, sound in speech which is beyond reproach..." (Titus 2:7-8). Both Old and New testaments provide biblical teachings on integrity.

The ICN Code of Ethics urges nurses to carry personal responsibility, use judgement for competent nursing care, and maintain accountability and standards of personal conduct to ensure professionally nursing practice. [2]

As Christian nurses we are encouraged to not only uphold integrity as a member of our profession, but we are also to model our actions and words after the Son of God. Jesus Christ lived an exemplary life replicating the virtues of God the Father.

We live out Christian integrity when our actions are congruent with what we say and believe. Some thoughts to reflect on when exploring integrity in your professional nursing are: Do you act, speak, and think in accordance with biblical teachings? How does your nursing practice replicate the teachings of Christ?

An excellent verse to guide our thoughts, actions and words is Philippians 4:8, "Finally, brothers and sisters, whatever is true, whatever is honorable, whatever is right, whatever is pure, whatever is lovely, whatever is commendable, if there is any excellence and if anything worthy of praise, think about these things."

Read: Titus 2:6-8

Reflect: Spend time thinking about the questions in the devotion.

Prayer: Oh, Holy Spirit guide us in living an exemplary life rooted in the ways of Jesus Christ. Amen.

NCFI Value: Celebrate Unity

By Carrie M. Dameron

For by one Spirit we were all baptized into one body (1 Corinthians 12:13).

One of the coolest things about NCFI is the unified voice of Christian nursing. I am not saying everyone is in agreement, nor that there is never conflict. Disagreements are to be expected with any family, group or organization, especially considering the diversity of cultures, experience, education, and personalities NCFI represent.

What I am speaking more about is the unity of Christ manifested by the lack of individual denominations. In other words, the question "What denomination do you belong to?" or "Where do you go to church?" has never come up in a conversation. I have attended two NCFI Congresses, a PACEA regional conference, International Board meetings, and numerous international conference calls and the focus has been on Christ-centered nursing.

We are all disciples and unique members of the body of Christ. We are unified for the same goal—equipping and encouraging Christian nurses to integrate Biblical principles and Christ-centered values. Which, by the way, is our mission![3] Ephesians 4:1-6 by Paul is a passage that contributes to our purpose in NCFI:

...urge you to walk in a manner worthy of the calling with which you have been called, with all humility and gentleness, with patience, bearing with one another in love, being diligent to keep the unity of the Spirit in the bond of peace. There is one body and one Spirit, just as you also were called in one hope of your calling; one Lord, one faith, one baptism, one God and Father of all who is over all and through all and in all.

Let's take the unity of Christ beyond NCFI and into our daily nursing practice, living out a commitment to focusing on commonalities. Instead of areas of dispute lets preserve our unified faith through the indwelling Spirit.

Read: 1 Corinthians 12:4-13

Reflect: Spend time reflecting how you can bring the unity of Christ to your nursing practice.

Prayer: Oh, Holy Spirit, guides us in being one body, one hope, one baptism and one calling, so that God may be glorified. Amen.

NCFI Value: Respect for All

By Carrie M. Dameron

with humility consider one another as more important than yourselves (Philippians 2:3).

The International Council of Nursing (ICN) states "respect for human rights, including the right to life, to dignity, and to be treated with respect." (2) This statement emphasizes the importance in providing dignified, respectful health care for the promotion of health, life and death.

As Christians our inclusive care for all patients and families is based on Galatians 3:28 "There is neither Jew nor Greek, there is neither slave nor free man, there is neither male nor female; for you are all one in Christ Jesus." We also have Romans 2:11 that guides us, "For, there is no partiality with God." A poignant reminder that God values all people.

As I reflect on respect as a Christian nursing value and the Lord's word, I see two challenges for nurses. The first is to not show partiality. Instead, reconcile within our self to provide the same love and grace to ALL persons. Christ encourages us to love them as we would love Him no matter what their religion, lifestyle, or criminal behavior. (Matthew 25:38-40)

Our second challenge is to respect our colleagues. I think the Lord's teaching is explicit with Philippians 2:3, "but with humility of mind regard one another as more important than yourselves." Whether we are providing nursing services, conducting a meeting, or educating others, the Lord challenges us to have a humble heart of servanthood to our colleagues, our patients, and their families.

Read: Philippians 2:1-5

Reflect: Which of the two challenges discussed is more personally difficult for you?

Prayer: Father God, I confess my pride in not caring for all Your children with humility and respect. Heal my heart and guide my hands. Amen.

D's & T's of Spiritual Warfare

By Carrie M. Dameron

We are destroying arguments and all arrogance raised against the knowledge of God, and we are taking every thought captive to the obedience of Christ. (2 Corinthians 10:5).

Just like a helmet can protect the vital structures of our brain. The helmet of salvation protects our mind from the enemy and various destructive thoughts (Ephesians 6:17). We can be deceived by confusing truths which impersonates lies. At times, we can lack insight or be devoid of the enemy devices. We can doubt the words and teachings of Jesus Christ. As well as distrust the work of the Holy Spirit in our lives and ministry. Through uncontrolled desires our thoughts can delve us into distractions, diversions and wayward detours. When disappointments tag along, we can get stuck in despair and distress. The Devil delights when devout Christians develop divisive, disruptive, and detrimental disobedience that defies the Divine.

Let's discontinue the work of the Devil and all those words that start with "d" and secure our mind with some thoughtful "t" words. Trust the truth of God's word and Christ' training found in both Testaments. Throw off temptation and terminate transgressions. Take time to be thankful and extol our Lord. With a transparent heart entreat Christ for protection and strength. Think, retain, and teach the tried-and-true texts that leads to virtuous thoughts. Strive for togetherness as a team while being thoughtful and attentive to all. Christians can tear apart the tormentor's enticements through the truth of the Word and the tenacity of their testimony.

Read: Ephesians 6:10-18

Reflect: Explore the devices of the Devil and discover which one tempts you the most?

Prayer: Father God, enable us to take every thought captive and stand firm against the devices of the evil one, so that our life and work brings glory to You. Amen.

Big Shoes of Leadership Includes Courage

By Carrie M. Dameron

Just as I have been with Moses, I will be with you; I will not desert you nor abandon you. Be strong and courageous. (Joshua 1:5-6).

Nurses are called into leadership positions and as Christians we should take these opportunities to have a greater influence towards Christ-centered nursing. At the same time, the big shoes of leadership can be daunting and overwhelming, causing many nurses to decline the opportunity.

When Joshua took Moses' place as Israel's leader, he had big shoes to fill. For 40 plus years, Moses had been the spokesman for God, the giver of the law, the indwelling presence of I AM, the warrior against Pharaoh's army, builder of a nation and caregiver of God's people. He not only directed the building of the tabernacle and guided them to daily sustenance of manna and doves, Moses governed the legal, political, and economic status of a nomadic, rebellious nation. How could Joshua, Moses' attendant, step into those huge leadership shoes?

Was Joshua frightened, worried, or anxious? Did he doubt his ability to be a leader that Israel would follow? Was he afraid of disappointing the Lord? Was he afraid to follow in the footsteps of his predecessor and never witness the fruition of his labors because of disobedience? These were big shoes to fill. Was Joshua ready for the challenge?

We have insight into Joshua's concerns and his need for assurance from the Lord. The Lord tells Joshua, "Be strong and courageous." In fact, the exhortation is repeated 3 times. (Joshua 1:6, 7, 9).

Today, the Lord speaks to you with the same encouragement: Be strong and courageous. The Lord will be with you, just as He was with Moses, Joshua, and other leaders.

Read: Joshua 1:1-9

Reflect: Have you declined a leadership position due to fear or concern about your abilities? If so, ask the Lord to open your heart to His courage in following His guidance.

Prayer: O' Lord, I will not be dismayed, nor tremble for You provide me with courage to lead. Amen.

Big Shoes of Leadership Includes a Plan for Success

By Carrie M. Dameron

This Book of the Law shall not depart from your mouth, but you shall meditate on it day and night, so that you may be careful to do according to all that is written in it; for then you will make your way prosperous, and then you will achieve success. (Joshua 1:8).

As Joshua stepped into the big shoes of leadership the Lord not only provided courage to lead, He provided a plan for success:

> *Just as I have been with Moses, I will be with you; I will not desert you nor abandon you...be careful to do according to all the Law which Moses My servant commanded you; do not turn from it to the right or to the left, so that you may achieve success wherever you go. This Book of the Law shall not depart from your mouth, but you shall meditate on it day and night, so that you may be careful to do according to all that is written in it; for then you will make your way prosperous, and then you will achieve success. Have I not commanded you? Be strong and courageous! Do not be terrified nor dismayed, for the LORD your God is with you wherever you go. (Joshua 1:5-9).*

The Lord provides us with the same plan He gave to Joshua:

- Don't Panic—trust God with all your misgiving, doubts, fears, etc., and He will guide your steps.
- Focus on the Word—like Moses, Joshua, Billy Graham and other great Christians, our strength is found in obedience to the Word.
- You have a Partner—God is faithful and is with you always.

Whether you have a title, position, or specific calling, all nurses are leaders. Our big shoes of leadership are probably not as big as Moses' shoes; but like Joshua you are to lead others following Christian principles.

Read: Joshua 1:1-9

Reflect: Which component of God's plan for Joshua's leadership is the most challenging for you?

Prayer: Holy Lord, just as You guided Joshua in filling in Big Shoes of leadership left behind by Moses, guide us in filling in Big Shoes of Leadership in our facilities, schools, and clinics. Amen.

Giving as Much as You Have Received

By Ishaku Izang

Now I say this, the one who sows sparingly will also reap sparingly, and the one who sows generously will also reap generously. (2 Corinthians 9:6).

This life is about giving and receiving. It is God that taught us how to give by giving us His one and only Son, the Lord Jesus Christ to be our Saviour and Redeemer (John 3:16).

The Scripture explicitly tells us that Jesus said, "It is more blessed to give than to receive" (Acts 20:35). We are also reminded that the more we give the more God will make grace abound in us (2 Corinthians 9:8); so that we will always be rich in good works for which we were created in Christ Jesus. (Ephesians 2:10).

Glory to God for calling us to serve Him in NCFI and as nurses. The Lord wants us to give as much as we have received from Him. He is not a task master, asking from us that which He has not given us. Instead, He only demands as much as He has given us. 2 Peter 1:3 says:

> *"for His divine power has granted us everything pertaining to life and godliness, through the true knowledge of Him who called us by His own glory and excellence."*

How much are you giving to your family? How much are you giving to your patients? How much are you giving to the church? How much are you giving to NCFI? Do you think you have given enough, or are you giving too much? Remember He says, "Truly I say to you, to the extent that you did not do for one of the least of these, you did not do to Me, either." (Matthew 25:45).

May we all be faithful to the Lord by giving back to Him through our service to one another what He has graciously given to us for the edification of the church which is His body. God bless you all.

Read: 2 Corinthians 9:6-11

Reflect: How much are you giving back to God?

Prayer: Father God, we praise and thank You and ask You to guide us in giving to You out of Your abundant blessings. Amen.

Proceed with Caution!

By Carrie M. Dameron

And do not be conformed to this world, but be transformed by the renewing of your mind, so that you may prove what the will of God is, that which is good and acceptable and perfect. (Romans 12:2).

"My Father is working until now, and I Myself am working." (John 5:17). This was Jesus' response to the Jewish leaders who had accused Him of violating the Sabbath by healing a lame man. Jesus repeatedly came up against the religious establishment for doing things in contrast to their rules--healing the blind, touching the unclean, and teaching the people. We can find ourselves in similar situations as Jesus. Especially, when the work of the Lord contrasts with health care and/or educational institutions policies. We may find ourselves coming up against the leadership.

For example: a group of Christian nurses want to meet weekly to pray, but the hospital administrators refuse to give them permission to use a room. What can the nurses do?

- Pray for the situation and the administrators while trusting the Lord to provide.
- Listen to the Holy Spirit who knows the work of the Father and the "will be done."
- Proceed with a heart filled with the grace and peace of Christ, knowing we represent Jesus to our colleagues and leaders.

This is just one example of how our Heavenly Father's work might contrast with the goals and plans of health care and educational facilities. When these occasions arise, we need an extra dose of discernment and guidance. Please recognize, this is not a call to be rebellious for rebellious sake. Instead, it is a reminder when conflict arises to proceed cautiously and discern the good, acceptable and perfect will of God for each individual situation. (Romans 12:2).

Read: Matthew 12:1-14

Reflect: Has there been a time when you proceeded with caution in attempting to implement God's truth in your workplace?

Prayer: Lord Jesus, give us a discerning heart to know when to stand firm in Your will or to submit to Your humble guidance. Amen.

Bold Prayer of Jabez for Nursing

By Gladys Altamirano Garrido

Now Jabez called on the God of Israel...And God brought about what he requested. (1 Chronicles 4:10).

We are accustomed to praying to God very humbly, almost timidly for a few things. We pray for forgiveness, healing, direction, guidance and even include requests for our friends. We don't dare to pray for what Jabez prayed for, nor in the way that he prayed:

> *"Oh, that You would greatly bless me and extend my border, and that Your hand might be with me, and that You would keep me from harm that it would not hurt me!" (1 Chronicles 4:10).*

Anyone who hears a prayer like this may be perplexed. We are not used to addressing God as Jabez did. One could even interpret Jabez' boldness as a lack of respect. The strangest thing about this prayer is that God heard it and responded! God gave Jabez what he asked for.

God's promise is, "Ask, and it will be given to you..." (Matthew 7:7). If God gave Jabez what he asked for, why won't God also give us what we ask for? If we ask Him to bless us and enlarge our territory, to sustain us with His hand and free us from evil so it won't hurt us, will God respond to us?

I think this prayer should stimulate us to boldly ask our Father to give us a blessing. We should also ask God to enlarge our territory in order to reach more nurses and midwives so that His name would be glorified through their work. In addition, with God's love, that nurses may minister to sick people or people needing physical, social or spiritual support.

We should also not forget to ask Him that His hand sustain us always and free us from evil. That He prevents us from maltreating sick people; from deceiving those around us; from lies that are often ready to come out of our lips; to protect us from failing people; that He free us from mistreating our colleagues and neighbors; and free us from doing our work badly. Finally, that God would guide us in the right way to give the best attention to those who need us.

If Jabez boldly asked and God answered Him. God can also "grant us our request" when we boldly ask Him.

Read: Matthew 7:7-11

Reflect: Do you have a bold need in nursing? Include it in the following prayer.

Prayer: God, I boldly come to You seeking ________________ so that I may care for your children entrusted to my care. Amen.

Be Ordinary

By Carrie M. Dameron

Take care not to practice your righteousness in the sight of people, to be noticed by them; otherwise you have no reward with your Father who is in heaven. (Matthew 6:1).

Recently, a leader of a missionary organization affiliated with my church gave an update. During his speech he said, "God has enough people doing the spectacular. He needs more people doing the ordinary." The truth of his words stuck with me. For even in nursing there are the spectaculars that we strive for in comparison to the ordinary. I see the spectacular in nursing as being big, bold and noticeable; whereas the ordinary in nursing is the small, quiet, and unseen interventions or tasks. The big and bold could be missionary trips, starting non-profit's, serving in leadership positions, and others. Whereas the ordinary is a conversation with a patient or family member, a warm coat for the homeless.

Jesus provides an excellent example of ordinary work with the Samaritan woman at the well. (John 4:1-26). Jesus stops to rest from His travels and to relieve His thirst. He notices a woman, alone at the well and begins a simple conversation with her. Well, we know the rest of the story. Through Jesus' ordinary act of drinking water and talking to one woman an entire town meets the long-awaited Messiah.

As we look through the Gospels, we see how the majority of Jesus' teachings and actions were ordinary conversations and one-on-one moments with individuals or small groups. Yes, He fed and taught large crowds. And yes, His torture and crucifixion were witnessed by hundreds. Yet, He taught His disciples to pray. He healed individuals and during His post-resurrection time He revealed Himself to a few men and women.

Read: Matthew 6:1-6

Reflect: Look for opportunities in nursing to be ordinary, so that the Holy Spirit can do the extraordinary and the Lord receives the glory.

Prayer: Lord, guide me in representing Jesus in the small, ordinary acts of loving Your children. Amen.

A Miracle Lullaby

By Carrie M. Dameron

I am the LORD, and there is no one else; There is no God except Me. (Isaiah 45:5).

I was recently at a hospital attending a conference where a brief, beautiful lullaby played every time a baby was born. The short 10 second tune notified all the staff, visitors, and patients throughout the hospital that a miracle had occurred. The Creator had breathed His life-giving Spirit into a new child.

As I sat in the conference, this beautiful lullaby(8) would attempt to interrupt the speakers with the brief proclamation of life. I kept thinking that each time the song played, possibly 3 or 4 times that morning, how many times do we take note of the miracles in our lives? Do we notice when the Lord has miraculously intervened on our behalf? If we do notice the Lord's hand in our life, do we stop our actions to pause and recognize with amazing wonder? Better yet, do we praise God for His unending grace that extends to each one of us personally throughout the day?

We can take untimely interruptions and praise God for His everlasting miracles in our world, celebrating His continuous abiding in our community and for His life-giving presence in each one of us. Let's also give the Holy Spirit permission to interrupt our lives, day or night, with opportunities to praise our Creator who works miracles every day!

I am the Lord, and there is no one else;
There is no God except Me.
I will arm you, though you have not known Me,
So that people may know from the rising to the setting of the sun
That there is no one besides Me.
I am the Lord, and there is no one else,
The One forming light and creating darkness,
Causing well-being and creating disaster;
I am the Lord who does all these things. (Isaiah 45:5-7).

Read: above verse

Reflect: What miracle have you been witness to? Take time to praise the Lord for His hand evident within our life?

Prayer: Lord, thank You for being the God of this universe, this planet and especially in my life. May Your name be forever praised. Amen.

On Our Knees: A Response to Disaster

By Carrie M. Dameron

For this reason I bend my knees before the Father, from whom every family in heaven and on earth derives its name, that He would grant you, according to the riches of His glory, to be strengthened with power through His Spirit in the inner self, (Ephesians 3:14-16).

We live during a unique time in history. Via the internet we our keenly aware of the various disasters occurring on the other side of the globe that impact a nation, city or region. It can be a typhoon in the Pacific, an earthquake in South America, or a terrorist attack in a large city. Instantaneously everyone is aware of the situation and can follow the updates through social media and global news.

As Christians we are a global family and have a simple, compassionate way to respond to the crisis occurring to our family members. We can pray. Every time you hear of a natural disaster, acts of terror or a breakout of illness and disease, you can bend your knees in prayer for our brothers and sisters around the globe. Here are some suggested prayer points:

- victims and families would come to know the Lord Jesus Christ.
- healing for the missing and/or wounded.
- the Lord would bring shelter and supplies.

I also suggest that you pray for the health care and emergency workers. As nurses, we know with every tragedy there are men and women whose work and calling puts them in harm's way and who work tirelessly giving of themselves for their patients. Pray for:

- strength and health to care for others.
- protect their families, so they may not worry.
- grace and love as they witness the tragedies and evil in our world.

Unfortunately, tragedy has become common place in our world today. As the Lord's workers we are the hands and heart of Jesus. His hands grow larger and His heart expands when our prayers join the Holy Spirit who intercedes for all of God's children.

Read: Ephesians 3:14-20

Reflect: Spend time praying for the most recent disaster.

Prayer: Father God, guide me in lifting up my Christian brothers and sisters around the globe who experience devastating suffering and those who provide health care services. Amen.

Conquer Self-Control Through Surrender

By Bulbuli Mollick

If we live by the Spirit, let's follow the Spirit as well. (Galatians 5:25).

Self-control is probably one of the hardest things to master. How often have we been defeated by a bad habit, a bad attitude, or a wrong mindset? We make promises to improve. We ask someone to hold us accountable. But deep inside, we know that we don't have the will or the ability to change. We can talk, we can plan, we can read books, and we can pray; but we still find it difficult to overcome and control many of the things that are inside us!

Thankfully, we know our God knows our weakness and He also knows the medicine which we need. The Bible says, "the fruit of the Spirit is love, joy, peace, patience, kindness, goodness, faithfulness, gentleness, self-control." (Galatians 5:22–23). The only way to gain self-control is by allowing the Holy Spirit to control us.

God is not nearly as concerned with our ability as He is with our surrender. In other words, our key focus is not *effort* but *surrender*—to live moment by moment submissively trusting in the Lord rather than in self. Paul says this is what it means to "walk by the Spirit." (Galatians 5:16).

Are you ready for a change? You can change, for God is in you and in us. As you surrender control to Him, He will help you bear the fruit of His likeness.

Read: Galatians 5:16-25

Reflect: What area of your life do you struggle to completely surrender to God?

Prayer: I am in need Lord of Your power so that I might change and grow. I surrender myself to You. Please help me to understand how to be submissive to You that I might be filled with Your Spirit. Amen.

The Two-Year Old "No"

By Carrie M. Dameron

My son, if you will receive my words And treasure my commandments within you, Make your ear attentive to wisdom, Incline your heart to understanding...Then you will understand the fear of the LORD And discover the knowledge of God. (Proverbs 2:1-2, 5).

Recently, I spent the day with both of my two-year old grandsons. Since they have different moms, I seldom see them together. The beautiful day was filled with bright sunshine, cool swimming, tasty ice cream and both two-year old's saying "No." In case you are unfamiliar with two-year old's, their favorite word is "No." They say no to everything. They even say "No" to things they want. They enjoy swimming, yet they will say "No" to swimwear. They enjoy eating ice cream, yet they will say "No" to getting out of the pool to eat the ice cream.

Later as I was reflecting on my afternoon filled with "No's," especially one filled with so much fun, I couldn't help but think of us as children of God. How many times do we say "No" to God? Do we say "No" even though a "Yes" will bring us pleasure and enjoyment? How many of us say "No" so firmly it is like a two-year old temper tantrum? Before you say "No" let me describe an adult two-year old temper tantrum. We say "No" so firmly we stop talking to God, we close our ears to hearing Him, refuse to read His word, start skipping church and justify our reason for saying "No."

All Christians can be tempted to say "No" to God; and I am sure we have all had adult temper-tantrums. They may not be the physical and screaming kind like a two-year old. Instead, they may be the sulking and withdrawal type. Just like a two-year old who needs the loving guidance of a parent to grow and mature; we need the loving guidance of our Heavenly Father to help us mature in our faith. He will guide us to say "Yes" to Jesus and His teachings and say "Yes" to the Kingdom of God. (Matthew 5:1-12).

Read: Matthew 5:1-12

Reflect: What areas of your life do you tend to say "No" to God?

Prayer: Be gracious to me, O God, according to Your faithfulness; According to the greatness of Your compassion wipe out my wrongdoings. Amen. (Psalm 51:1).

Be Hesed

By Carrie M. Dameron

He [the LORD] has told you, O man, what is good; And what does the LORD require of you. But to do justice, to love kindness, and to walk humbly with your God? (Micah 6:8).

Scripture teaches us to "put on kindness" like a garment to wear (Colossians 3:12); yet we can fairly quickly change our garment of kindness into selfishness and pride. We also learn that the Holy Spirit working within us brings out the fruit of kindness (Galatians 5:22); yet sometimes our fruit is less sincere and under-ripe. Throughout Scripture we see how the kindness of God is demonstrated to us through extending kindness to others.

In Micah we are instructed that we are to "love kindness" or "mercy" in the KJV. The Hebrew word is transliterated into '*hesed*' and is translated to mercy, goodness, faithfulness and frequently used to describe God as lovingkindness.[(9)] Notice how Moses, the writer of Exodus, described the LORD's presence and proclamation.

> *Then the LORD passed by in front of him and proclaimed, "The LORD, the LORD God, compassionate and merciful, slow to anger, and abounding in faithfulness (hesed) and truth; who keeps faithfulness (hesed) for thousands" (Exodus 34:6).*

In other words, '*hesed*' is an attribute or character of God's presence. Thus, kindness is our presence, our personality, and the essence of our spirit. *Hesed* is not based on a mood, emotion, action or attitude. Instead, it should be so greatly ingrained within us that it naturally spills out continuously onto others.

Read: Exodus 34:4-9

Reflect: How can you embrace *Hesed* as an essence of your sprit instead of an action "to do"?

Prayer: O Lord, indwell within me through Your living Spirit hesed, so that I may be lovingkindness to others. Amen.

Humility towards Men & Women

By Carrie M. Dameron

He [the LORD] has told you, O man, what is good; And what does the LORD require of you. But to do justice, to love kindness, and to walk humbly with your God? (Micah 6:8).

Thankfully, we need to look no further than to Jesus Christ to demonstrate how to "walk humbly with our God." We readily think of the humble self-sacrifice Christ provided for our redemption (Philippians 2:5-11); additionally, Jesus demonstrated His supreme love for mankind by humbly serving others. Andrew Murray's "Humility"(10) exclaims that our humility with God is demonstrated by loving our neighbor through sacrificial service to others:

> "It is easy to think we humble ourselves before God: humility towards men will be the only sufficient proof that our humility before God is real; that humility has taken up its abode in us; and become our very nature; that we actually, like Christ, have made ourselves of no reputation." (p. 12).

Further, a perusal of Murray's work reflects our Savior's meek and lowly heart (Matthew 11:29) while revealing a few excellent tips:

- Pray for the Holy Spirit to wash us afresh with the humility of Christ.
- Explore new ways to honor others above ourselves at home and work.
- Bear upon ourselves the failings and sins of fellow-Christians for the unity of peace.
- Look upon every person as a child of God with honor and preference as an esteemed son/daughter of the King.
- Praise God most fervently when others are preferred and blessed.

May we seek to live like the Apostle Paul in saying through both word and deed, I am "the very least of all the saints" (Ephesians 3:8).

Read: Philippians 2:5-11

Reflect: Which one from the above tips on humility is the most challenging to live out?

Prayer: Oh Lord, only through daily surrender can I ever grasp the identity of being the 'least of all the saints.' Make me humble, Lord. Amen.

Let the Word Guide the New Year

By Martha Fernández Moyano

Sustain me according to Your word, that I may live; (Psalm 119:116).

At the beginning of each new year, we make new plans to renew our strength. We are sure that nothing will stop our new plans. Yet, when we begin to take those first steps of change or our dreams begin to be realized, doubts arise within us. A fear or a feeling that something bad happens or we lack strength and resources. We begin to waver.

What seemed safe and close now seems far and impossible. What we once wanted to accomplish and what we believed was so urgent, has now become routine or secondary to our daily activities. Just after the first month of the year our plans and objectives are diluted, and we are already doing the same things that we do every year. Where did our plans go? Where did our resolve go to make those changes?

The Word of God has many resources to sustain you in everything you propose new this year:

Forces: " 'Not by might nor by power, but by My Spirit,' says the LORD of armies." (Zechariah 4:6).
Sustenance: "Cast your burden upon the LORD and He will sustain you; He will never allow the righteous to be shaken." (Psalm 55:22).
Worries: "...cast all your anxiety on Him, because He cares about you." (1 Peter 5:7)
Overcoming fear: "For I am the LORD your God, who takes hold of your right hand, Who says to you 'Do not fear, I will help you.' " (Isaiah 41:13).
Security: " 'For I know the plans I have for you,' declares the LORD, 'plans for prosperity and not for disaster to give you a future and a hope.' " (Jeremiah 29:11).

May this be the best year of our lives, because "If, God is for us, who is against us? ...Who will separate us from the love of Christ..." Nothing! Thanks to my Lord. (Romans 8:31, 36)

Read: Romans 8:31-36

Reflect: Use one of the above verses or another Scripture to secure your plans for the new year.

Prayer: Lord teach me to plan my life, according to Your will. Remove and add what You think is best for my life and thus fulfill the purpose You have for me this year. Amen.

Responding to Conflict

By Swee Eng Goh

For the fountain of life is with You; In Your light we see light. (Psalm 36:9).

So often we mull over, moan over the wrongs that people have done to us. People like family members, church leaders, members, colleagues and bosses who have misbehaved toward us replay in our mind. Choosing this habit of thinking will produce a toxic mind set which will only rob us of the joy, peace and righteousness in the Holy Spirit. The thoughts will also impact our health and overall life.

One way to encourage you on the journey of a transformational way to renew the mind is to read and meditate on the 12 verses found in Psalm 36. In my New King James Version, the title of this Psalm reads "Man's Wickedness and God's Perfections."

David, the writer, states the psalm is an oracle. In other words, a divine utterance delivered to man as an answer to a request for guidance. David revealed his heart and the transgression of the wicked in the first 4 verses or a 1/3 of the psalm. However, he spent the next verses 5 through 12, focusing on God's character: mercy, faithfulness, righteousness, judgments, lovingkindness, provider, fountain of life and his response to the wicked. This is 2/3 of the psalm written in response to the transgression of the wicked.

We can choose to dwell on previous bad behaviors, or the wrongs done to us. Or we can choose to dwell more on God, who He is and what He has done and can do for us. Like the psalmist, we can choose to dwell on who God is and His actions, which is an important process in renewing the mind.

Read/Reflect: Read Psalm 36 and take note on how David focuses on the righteous character and actions of God.

Prayer: Oh, Lord forgive me when I hold on to the wickedness of the world instead of releasing them to Your righteous actions. Amen.

Grace & Mercy—Kids Style!

By Carrie M. Dameron

The LORD is gracious and compassionate; Slow to anger and great in mercy. (Psalm 145:8).

My 9-year-old grandson came to my house for the weekend with a cloud hanging over his head. His mother had received an email from his teacher stating he had misbehaved in class and had repeated episodes of incomplete homework. Since, my husband and I would care for him for the weekend, we were responsible for deciding on how to proceed with his punishment. We decided that our grandson would spend the weekend "making up his homework." His punishment for his bad classroom behavior would be "no TV, no phone games, and no outside play."

As the weekend went on, we noticed our young grandson taking responsibility for his actions and working hard to make-up his homework. So, we took the opportunity to teach our growing young man about two important attributes of God--grace and mercy. I explained that grace is where we get something that we don't deserve. For example, since he had a good attitude towards his punishment and had made up his homework, we dispensed grace and let him watch a movie with the family.

Through the weekend, we laughed with him as he tried to figure out if he wanted grace or mercy, for at times he wasn't sure. He just wanted to watch TV or play a game on his phone. So, we would remind him: grace is getting something you don't deserve; whereas mercy is not getting something you do deserve. For example, he probably deserved stiffer consequence for his bad behavior, like a weekend filled with chores, a week without "electronics" or some other stiffer penalty.

On Sunday evening, when we passed our grand parenting responsibilities back to his mother, he proudly told his mother about his new word. "Grandma and papa gave me grace which means I watched a movie; or maybe mercy. I am not sure which one it is. But my sister got to pick out the movie, which was okay."

We weren't sure whether his future would be filled with grace, mercy, or justice; for Mom had yet to dole out her consequences.

Read: Psalm 145

Reflect: Are you more conscious of the grace of God or the mercy of God?

Prayer: Oh, Lord Your lovingkindness is everlasting, and Your mercies are new every morning. Amen (Psalm 136; Lamentations 3:3).

Change Negative Attitudes to Positive Part I

By Bulbuli Mollick

Watch over your heart with all diligence, For from it flow the springs of life. (Proverbs 4:23).

A positive attitude contributes to success in life more than anything else. What can we do if our mind is bogged down by negative attitudes that limit our success? You and I can change our attitudes with God's help. Here are some suggestions:

Understand the power of attitude. If we allow negative attitudes (such as anxiety, envy, anger, bitterness, or pride) to grab hold of our mind, those attitudes will lead us to make negative decisions. But if we choose to develop and maintain positive attitudes, our life will become positive as a result. Even when we encounter challenges and tragedies, we will be able to deal with them successfully when we choose to approach life with positive attitudes. Keep in mind that changing negative attitudes to positive ones isn't an instant event; it's a lifelong process that requires perseverance. We should ask God to help us each moment of each day and study Jesus' life. By reading the Bible each day we will see how Jesus is the ultimate example of how to live in a fallen world with positive attitudes.

Examine your soul. Ask God to help you take an honest look inside your soul to identify what specific types of negative attitudes are lurking inside, such as: pride, fear, anger, sadness, jealousy, doubt, dislike, bitterness, and low self-esteem (Mark 7:21-23). Confess each of the negative attitudes to God and repent of them; inviting God to transform you from the inside out. Going forward, each time you become aware of an unhealthy, negative thought in your mind, give it to God in prayer and ask the Holy Spirit to renew your mind so you can clearly think the way the Lord wants you to think.

Self-examination and submitting thoughts to the Lord will help you develop positive attitudes that will fill your soul regularly.

Read: Mark 7:14-23

Reflect: Spend some time examining your soul and looking for negative attitudes

Prayer: Oh, God, give me a steadfast heart so that I will sing Your praises. Amen. (Psalm 57:7).

Change Negative Attitudes to Positive Part II

By Bulbuli Mollick

The heart of the righteous ponders how to answer, But the mouth of the wicked pours out evil things. (Proverbs 15:28).

In addition to recognizing how a negative attitude can impact our lives and the importance of examining our soul, we should also review how we can respond to negative situations.

Respond rather than react to unexpected change. Change will sometimes surprise us. We may be drawn into a crisis especially when that change is negative. Whenever that happens, avoid reacting negatively and instead deliberately decide to respond positively.

Keep in mind that we can't control situations or people, but we can choose how we will respond to them. Ask God to give you four key gifts to help you have a positive response to unexpected changes: hope, faith in Him, a clear vision of what He wants us to do next, and the energy to do what He wants us to do. Whenever it's possible for us to change troubling circumstances or relationships, make the effort to do so. Whenever we can't change them, ask God to give us the peace and encouragement we need to deal with them.

If we will read the following verses, accept them and faithfully maintain their work then, of course, our attitude will be changed: Galatians 5:16-20, Proverbs 15:30, Psalm 16:11.

Remember that "All Scripture is inspired by God and profitable for teaching, for rebuke, for correction, for training in righteousness; so that the man or woman of God may be fully capable, equipped for every good work. (2 Timothy 3:16-17). Changing our negative attitude is possible through God's words.

Read: Review the cited verses

Reflect: Which one of the four gifts discussed can assist you in responding positively to a negative situation?

Prayer: Thank you, Father God, that Your word guides us in equipping us for all circumstances we face on earth. Amen.

Problem + Solution = Faith Lesson

By Carrie M. Dameron

For the LORD gives wisdom; From His mouth come knowledge and understanding. (Proverbs 2:6).

In Acts 6:1-5 we read how the Hellenistic Jewish were being left out of the daily allotment of food for their widows. So, the Jews made a complaint to the disciples about the unfairness of distribution.

> *"So the twelve summoned the congregation of the disciples and said, 'It is not desirable for us to neglect the word of God in order to serve tables. Instead, brothers and sisters, select from among you seven men of good reputation, full of the Spirit and of wisdom, whom we may put in charge of this task. But we will devote ourselves to prayer and to the ministry of the word.' "(verses 2-5).*

The early church had experienced rapid growth after Pentecost. I imagine the disciples were pulled in every direction and worked 24/7 to facilitate believer's maturity while extending the gospel to others. A closer look at this passage reveals how the Lord used this opportunity to not only provide a solution, but to also guide and teach the early church valuable lessons still relevant for us today:

- When there is conflict or complaining, instead of ignoring the problem or labeling the spokesperson a complainer; listen and understand the concerns. It was only after the complaint that the disciples recognized their priority as leaders—not to "serve tables or distribute food."
- Seek the Lord for the solution. The problem and/or the solution may be an opportunity for the Holy Spirit to emphasize an important biblical truth in our personal and ministry life. Thankfully, the omniscience God of miracles provides a solution while guiding us in living-out His will more fully.
- Finally, no matter how busy our work in nursing becomes, ministry is sustained by the two-fold, intertwined process of the word of God and prayer. We can get pulled in multiple directions and forget to take the time to pray and study God's word.

Seek the Lord for the faith lesson found in both the problem and the solution in our workplace.

Read: Acts 6:1-5

Reflect: Next time you have a workplace problem, seek the Lord and see how he builds your faith through providing the solution.

Prayer: Oh Lord, prompt us to bring Your extraordinary wisdom and understanding to all aspects of our life. Amen.

Communicate Like Jesus

By Swee Eng Goh

In the beginning was the Word, and the Word was with God and the Word was God...And the Word became flesh, and dwelt among us, and we saw His glory, glory as of the only Son from the Father, full of grace and truth. (John 1:1, 14).

Nowadays with the use of emoji on handheld devices, the challenge to say how we feel, or think has been made easier. Maybe we rely too much on emojis instead of learning to communicate with pleasant words. When God wanted to communicate, He sent His Son, the Word, who became flesh and dwelt among us. (John 1:1,14).

Thomas Kempis (1380-1471), a follower of Christ who lived in dark time, regarded meditation on the life of Christ of highest importance. Like Kempis, I have started reading the Gospel of John to glean ways Christ communicates in different situations and with different people. For example, Jesus communicated very differently with Nicodemus than with the Samaritan woman. With Nicodemus, He used words and concepts that a learned religious man could dialogue with, like "'You must be born again.'" (John 3:7). With the Samaritan woman, Jesus communicated in such a way as to make her curious for the living water while using affirmative ways to say, "You have correctly said, 'I have no husband.' " (John 4:17-18). Wow, it is difficult for most of us to say to a stranger something about his or her controversial personal life.

We can learn to rescript our words with people. I believe it must be intentional and will take practice. As you read the Gospels, focus your meditation on looking for any aspect of Christ's life. Ask God to show you, by looking at the Gospels, how Jesus communicated with others. Journal it down and add comments as the Lord shows you or teaches you something. These meditations can become raw materials to teach biblical truth in different settings whether in nursing or personal life. Let us learn together how to communicate like Christ.

Read/Reflect: Complete the above activity with your favorite reading in the Gospels.

Prayer: Thank you Jesus, that Your life is an example for us to live by. Amen

Lost Joy

By Martha Fernández Moyano

For the joy of the LORD is your refuge. (Nehemiah 8:10).

There are things we tend to lose, right? Simple items like a pen, glasses, cell phone, or a piece of paper with an important annotation. Some would say Christians can lose "our hope." But there is something that we all can easily lose, especially Christian nurses. It is our joy.

On Sundays we leave church joyfully excited to serve the Lord. Yet, as soon as we arrive at the hospital, there is bad news. A change in our work plans, the absence of a colleague, work overload, and a host of other things make us lose our Sunday joy.

Romans 14:17 says: "for the kingdom of God is not eating and drinking, but righteousness and peace and joy in the Holy Spirit." Joy is the natural outflow of following Christ. While we are living during these difficult days, we are reminded of Lamentations 5:15 "The joy of our hearts has ceased; Our dancing has been turned into mourning." It seems like the complaint and the hopelessness attempts to overwhelm us. Here is a list of things that can steal our joy:

<u>An unbalanced schedule</u>: nurses tend to overload their schedule and then frustration comes when we are unable to complete everything.
<u>Selfishness</u>: when we want to only receive the benefits of our profession and not deliver the added value to our work, such as love and mercy.
<u>Unused talents</u>: when we do not use all our talents, our gifts, abilities and fall into a routine. We must use all that God has given us to enrich our work.
<u>Unconfessed sin</u>: inside we know that we have unresolved things, such as not accepting a colleague, feeling upset with our supervisor, jealousy, anger, strife, and others. We need to confess sin to the Lord and ask His help in looking at our colleagues with the eyes of Christ.
<u>Unresolved conflict</u>: like negativity, gossip, bad humor, and bitterness steals the joy of the Lord.
<u>A malnourished spirit</u>: we can only face all these things that rob us of joy, when we strengthen our spirit with the Word of God and consistent prayer.

Stay vigilant so that you can always be dancing with joy before our Lord.

Read: Psalm 33

Reflect: Look and pray over the above list finding points in your life that has stolen your joy.

Prayer: Oh, Lord, restore to me the joy of Your salvation and sustain me with a willing spirit." (Psalm 51:12).

How We Grieve the Holy Spirit

By Swee Eng Goh

Do not grieve the Holy Spirit of God, by whom you were sealed for the day of redemption. All bitterness, wrath, anger, clamor and slander must be removed from you, along with all malice. (Ephesians 4:30-31).

An incident at work between two Christian co-workers brought to my mind the teaching found in Ephesians 4:30-31. I reflected on my own responses in anger towards others, rightly or wrongly; and how I too would have grieved the Holy Spirit if I continued to hold on to that anger.

According to the dictionary, 'grief' is deep and poignant distress caused by or as if by bereavement [12] In medical terms, there is no consensus on the defining features that would distinguish normal and pathological 'grief', it is generally accepted that 'grief' becomes pathological when the reactions are excessive, prolonged, or unresolved. In counselling, the grieving one understands that the loss of a close person, loss of job or loss of a dream can be devastating. The Lord allows us to go through grief and in this, we can identify with Jesus who is acquainted with grief, and even borne our griefs, a man of sorrows (Isaiah 53:3,4). Christ' humanity brings us closer to Him and we can accept our human frailty of experiencing grief because He also experienced it. God has emotions but He is transcendent, beyond our comprehension.

The Bible uses the word "grieve or grieved" 37 times in the New King James translation with both the Old and New Testament citing how God or the Holy Spirit was grieved. In Genesis 6:6, "So the LORD was sorry that He had made mankind on the earth, and He was grieved in His heart" tells us that God is grieved when man rebuffed His covenantal love in sin and disobedience. God was also grieved when the Israelites rebelled in the desert under Moses' leadership. God's anguished response to sin is evidenced in two main ways: divine judgment and compassion for the sinner. Because God is holy, He has to judge sin, but He offers compassion and salvation for sinners in the process.

May we be very conscious that the Holy Spirit can be grieved through our actions, speech, and our attitudes in our day-to-day life responses.

Read: Ephesians 4:25-5:2

Reflect: How have you grieved the Holy Spirit with your words and/or actions?

Prayer: Lord, teach us how to live and walk by the Spirit. Amen

The Cross-Cultural Mission Field at Our Workplace

By Carrie M. Dameron

Sing to the LORD, all the earth; Proclaim good news of His salvation from day to day. Tell of His glory among the nations, His wonderful deeds among all the peoples. (1 Chronicles 16:23-24).

Throughout Scripture we see the Apostles bringing the love of God and grace of Christ to various cultures and religions. The most dramatic is Philip, who was led by the Holy Spirit to travel to a specific road in Gaza to meet with an Ethiopian court official. (Acts 8:27-40). He explains the passage of Isaiah and then proceeds to lead the official to salvation and baptism.

Reaching out cross-culturally to bring the love and grace of Christ to others, doesn't have to be a call to the mission field. We can bring the love of God and grace of Christ cross-culturally to those within our spheres of influence. We can connect one-on-one with people around us and explore their religion, country of origin or ethnicity. Here are some ideas to get started:

- Take extra time to talk with a patient or their family exploring their home life.
- Have lunch with a coworker and learn about their religious practices.
- Connect with a student and discover their cultural traditions.
- Invite someone to a Christian festival (Christmas, Easter, etc.).

As Christians we have the tendency to spend time with only Christians and like-minded individuals. With the influx of immigrants in most nations and the diversity of global travelers, we have an opportunity to learn about various cultures and religions right within our work environment. As we take time to pray for our coworkers, our patients and/or our students, we can spread the love God has for all His children through our conversations and professional relationships.

Read: Acts 8:27-40

Reflect: Reach out to a coworker from a different religion or culture.

Prayer: Father God, give me a heart for all Your children. Even those who seem the farthest away from Your Son and His grace. Amen.

A Song in my Heart

By Carrie M. Dameron

"Sing to Him a new song; Play skillfully with a shout of joy." (Psalm 33:3).

I have a granddaughter who is constantly singing. When we are driving in the car, hanging out at home, or walking to the park, she is singing a song. Many times, she repeats the chorus or refrain to a recent pop song over and over. I enjoy listening to her sing even when it is annoying to her older brother. At times I do have to have her tone it down, especially if her singing borders on the edge of screaming. The beautiful thing about her singing is it comes out naturally; in fact, she was born with a song-in-her-heart. I remember when she was just a few days old, holding her and she was humming along. Since she had just left the Lord presence, I asked her softly, "Are you singing the songs of angels?"

I share this with you, not just to brag as a loving grandmother, but also to remind us that we can all have a song in our heart. The natural song or verse in our heart overflows from a heart and spirit filled with the goodness of God. We sing praises of His wonderfulness and out of gratefulness to Him and all His provisions. Here are a few verses that speak of having a song in your heart:

- "singing and making melody in your hearts to the Lord always giving thanks to God the Father for all things" (Ephesians 5:19-20).
- "Let the word of Christ richly dwell within you...singing with thankfulness in your hearts to God." (Colossians 3:16).
- "Is anyone in good cheerful? He is to sing praises" (James 5:13).
- "My heart is steadfast, God; I will sing, I will sing praises, also with my soul." (Psalm 108:1).
- "The LORD is my strength and my shield; My heart trusts in Him, and I am helped; Therefore, my heart triumphs, And with my song I shall thank Him." (Psalm 28:7).

Unlike my granddaughter I am not naturally musical, however through the Holy Spirit, I can always find a song in my heart.

Read: Psalm 108:1-5

Reflect: Take some time this week and put a song in your heart. If you are naturally musically, invent your own melody of praise; otherwise find a favorite hymn, song, or refrain to fill your heart with the Lord's praises.

Prayer, O Lord, may my sacrifice of praise and thanksgiving ascend into Your throne room and be acceptable unto You. Amen.

Dispel Ungodly Beliefs

By Bulbuli Mollick

But you are A CHOSEN PEOPLE, A royal PRIESTHOOD, A HOLY NATION, A PEOPLE FOR GOD'S OWN POSSESSION, so that you may proclaim the excellencies of Him who has called you out of darkness into His marvelous light; (1 Peter 2:9).

Here are a few wonderful reminders of who we are in Christ:

- John 1:12: "But as many as received Him, to them He gave the right to become children of God"
- John 15:1, 15: "I am the true vine, and my Father is the vinedresser. No longer do I call you slaves, for the slave does not know what his master is doing; but I have called you friends, for all things that I have heard from My Father I have made known to you."
- Roman's 8:28: "And we know that God causes all things to work together for good to those who love God, to those who are called according to His purpose."

We know that we are chosen by Christ, we are His children. He loves us and has called us for His purpose. He gave us everything and whatever we need. But sometimes we break our faith in Him. Sometimes we want to be free and live ungodly beliefs. So, how can we get free from ungodly beliefs and live in the light of God's truth?

- Identify and write down the problem.
- Forgive the people who have wounded us.
- Ask the Holy Spirit for a revelation of truth.
- Write down a godly belief.
- Proclaim the new godly belief for 30 days.

Ungodly beliefs have the power to rob us. Godly beliefs have the power to give us mercy, grace and favor while reminding us of who we are in Christ.

Read: 1 Peter 2:9-12

Reflect: Follow the above steps to dispel an ungodly belief.

Prayer: Lord Jesus, we are Your chosen servants called to a new purpose. Guide us in aligning our heart and spirit with Your truth. Amen.

Our Amazing Hands

By Carrie M. Dameron

Make it your ambition to lead a quiet life and attend to your own business and work with your hands (1 Thessalonians 4:11).

Guided by two strong arms our hands collaborate together yet work independently. Each hand contains 4 bones for each finger and 3 bones for the thumb. Along with bones in the palm and the intrinsic bones of wrist we have 29 bones in each hand. A mesh of tendons and muscles provide dexterity for the multiple functions of gripping, fanning, and arching. Tough for manual work, but sensitive to interpret dots on a line for reading braille. Gentle to caress and touch, while quick and responsive for pianists and guitarists. The ridges on the fingertips have unique signature loops and curves that create individual prints precise to each individual human. A hand can create a fist for fighting, hold a cup for drinking and gently cradle an infant's head. Hands can be raised in worship, clasped in prayer and extended to one another in unity and partnership.

As nurses we frequently wash our hands to prevent infections, hold patient hands for comfort and strength, and bring many hands together to share our workload. We have used our hands to wipe tears, cleanse wounds, apply ointments, and assess temperature. With the increasing complexity of computers and devices, we use our hands to program pumps, manage devices, document medical care and connect with colleagues through cell phones, tablets and computers.

Praise God for His wonderful, creatively designed hands. Thank Him for the blessing to have hands that can fulfill many functions, for we know of people around the world who lose one or both hand(s) and/or the many functions of their hand(s) due to congenital, trauma, illness, or disease.

Take a moment to care for your hands. They work hard and are an important nursing tool.

Read: In the Bible do a word search for "hand" and explore the various functions of the Lord's hands.

Reflect: Connect with a colleague or group and perform a "Blessing of the Hands" Ceremony. [16]

Prayer: Thank you Lord for the work of Your hands in creating my hands so that I in turn can assist You in Your work. Amen.

How to be an NCFI Hero

By Carrie M. Dameron

[Saul] took food and was strengthened...for several days he was with the disciples who were at Damascus. (Acts 9:19).

Recently my Missions Pastor taught how church members can provide support for the spiritual leaders of our church. The teaching was based on Acts 9:19-31, where many unnamed believers or biblical Heroes provided various types of support for Saul (Paul), an up-and-coming church leader. As I listened to the teaching, I knew the teaching was relevant and applicable to NCFI. So, I took the outline and adapted it for NCFI ministry. For just as these unnamed believers in Acts are Heroes, so is everyone who supports NCFI. The next series of devotions show how you can be a NCFI Hero and provide much needed support for the leadership team.

The first spiritual support NCFI Heroes can provide is prayer. Not just general prayer, but specifically protection from the evil one. (Matthew 6:13). Jesus emphasized the importance of protection throughout the Gospels. John 17:15, "I am not asking You to take them out of the world, but to keep them from the evil one." As NCFI leaders strive to encourage and support Christian nurses around the world we are confronted by the schemes of the devil who seeks to thwart our work regionally and globally. The leadership team is also at risk of personal onslaught from Satan who plots to destroy our personal faith and professional lives.

Of course, it goes without saying we also need general prayer. **The NCFI Prayer Guide** is published every quarter on the NCFI website. https://ncfi.org/resources/prayer-guides/ The guide is a day-to-day list of prayer needs and praise reports from our member countries and global contacts, in addition to organizational requests. It also lists the International Board Members, leaders and NG contacts who seek your prayer support. Remember, the work of NCFI is dependent upon the faithful prayer of our NCFI Heroes.

Read: Acts 9:19-31

Reflect: Commit to regularly praying for NCFI and global Christian nursing.

Prayer: Oh, Lord we know You are faithful to strengthen us and protect us from the evil one; direct our hearts toward Your love and the steadfastness of Your Son. Amen. (2 Thessalonians 3:3,5).

The Purpose of NCFI Heroes

By Carrie M. Dameron

And the word of the Lord was being spread through the whole region. (Acts 13:49).

The Purpose of NCFI is to connect Christian nurses around the world, equipping them to live out their faith in professional practice. This is accomplished by guiding Christian nurses in integrating biblical principles and Christ-centered values in clinical practice, leadership, education and research with the following Aims or focus:

- Encourage Christian nurses and nursing students to live out their faith in
- compassionate professional practice.
- Deepen the spiritual life and cultural awareness of Christian nurses and nursing students around the world.
- Promote friendship, communication, connection and collaboration among Christian nurses worldwide.
- Support Regional NCFI Councils (Committee) and National NCF organizations in their ministry with nurses.
- Empower Christian nurses to examine and apply Scripture as it relates to professional practice.
- Equip and support the development of Christian nurse leaders around the world.
- Represent Christian nursing in the global nursing and healthcare arena. http://ncfi.org/about-ncfi/

We praise and thank the Lord when one person in one country seeks out NCFI. We know the Lord's work is going out. This is a tough time to be a Christian, especially in health care and nursing. Thus, if we can encourage one nurse in one country, we are successful.

Thank you for being an NCFI Hero. I pray for the Lord to guide your hands/heart in supporting the leadership team and know he will bless you.

Read: Colossians 1:9-14

Reflect: Review the above list and pray how you can personally support the mission and aims of NCFI.

Prayer: Lord God, continue to guide NCFI in encouraging Christian nurses across the globe. Amen.

The Benefits of being an NCFI Hero

By Carrie M. Dameron

So the church throughout all Judea, Galilee and Samaria enjoyed peace, as it was being built up; and as it continued in the fear of the Lord and in the comfort of the Holy Spirit, it kept increasing. (Acts 9:31).

In the previous devotions we have explored how you can become a NCFI Heroes by supporting the NCFI leadership team. We looked at not only using the NCFI Prayer Guide, but a specific need for protection from the evil one. Then we shared how NCFI needs specific provisions of people. Finally, we reached out and reminded everyone how ministry workers need positive affirmations. A kind word, a simple gesture can encourage the leadership team in their amazing work.

In this devotion we will explore the benefits of being an NCFI Hero. We see in Acts 9:31 the benefits or fruit of the believers' support of Saul. As the believers supported and encouraged the up-and-coming church leader, there was a bountiful harvest of spiritual and physical blessings.

They enjoyed a time of peace apart from difficult personal circumstances (Philippians 4:7). Instead, their peace was deep serenity rooted in God. Notice also the believers' faith was being built up as they witnessed and participated in God's active Kingdom work. While experiencing the intimate experience of the Holy Spirit, the believers had an increasing reverence and respect for the Lord.

Finally, notice how the benefits were not just for certain people, like Paul and Barnabas. Rather, the benefits were experienced by the body of believers through all regions of the early Christian church. It was not just one church, one community, nor just under one leader. Instead, the transformation in the community was experienced by every believer.

As you continue to be NCFI Heroes that support the leadership of NCFI, the change is not just for you. Instead, the life transformation from participating in the work of Kingdom is exponentially impacting your community, nation, region and around the globe. Wow!

Read: Acts 9:19-31

Reflect: How has being supportive of NCFI impacted your faith and/or nursing practice?

Prayer: Oh, Lord, we rejoice in the fruit of Your work and the expansion of Your Kingdom among nurses. Amen.

Lord Save Me!

By Carrie M. Dameron

[Peter] cried out, saying "Lord, save me!" (Matthew 14:30).

Many of us our familiar with Peter, who after seeing Jesus walk across the Sea of Galilee, stepped out of the boat and walked on water with Jesus. At some point in His miraculous steps, Peter became frightened and began sinking into the water and cries out to Jesus, "Lord, save me!" (Matthew 14:23-33). These 3 simple words form the basis of the most powerful, simplest prayer. A simple prayer that can guide us in teaching our patients how to pray.

First, we guide our patients in calling out to the only one who can help them, "Lord." We don't pray to a cosmic force, an unknown god nor one of the many god's worshiped in other religions. Instead, we call out to the Almighty God through our Savior.

Second, is the action verb "save." This simple 4 letter word communicates so much of the human experience. An English dictionary gives the following definitions for "save": rescue from danger or from pain and fear; spare the individual from suffering, anxiety, or the unknown; and stop the spread of illness, infection, or cancer.[(17)] And of course, the verb "save" is also used to communicate the need for forgiveness and a Savior (Luke 19:10; Romans 10:13).

The final word "me" is more than a personal pronoun. It is an intimate identification as a child of God. That the Lord of Heaven, the Creator of the Universe knows each hair on our head, cells in our bodies, and days of our lives.

Together, "Lord, save me." is a simple prayer that anyone can learn. It communicates the magnitude needs of humanity calling out to the only power able to change the situation. Next time your patients or clients are new Christians, experiencing pain or discomfort, or too distraught to pray, teach them this simple prayer. Then you can rest in confidence knowing the Lord will answer their prayer.

Read: Matthew 14:23-33

Reflect: What would you like the Lord to save you from? Fill in the prayer below.

Prayer: Lord, save me from __________! (fill in the blank) Amen.

What Do You Have to Give?

By Ishaku Izang

Peter, along with John, looked at him intently and said, "Look at us!" (Acts 3:4).

The ministry of Jesus to the world is to tell the world that His presence and power is still available in the life of His followers (believers). Today Jesus is looking for Christian nurses through whom and in whom He will display His presence and power to impact their patients, colleagues and their workplace.

In Acts 3:1-5, we read the beginning ministry of Jesus Christ working through the disciples. Peter and John were going to the temple for prayer. Even though other temple goers neglected the blind man, Peter and John did not look away. While other nurses can afford to look away and abandon the suffering and plight of patients, Christian nurses are called to look and respond. We may be tempted to say, "I am too busy." Or, "I am going for my church program." Or, "Others can do it." Proverbs 21:13 says, "One who shuts his ear to the outcry of the poor Will also cry himself, and not be answered."

Whereas the blind man expected silver or gold from Peter and John, they had none. However, they had the power of Jesus. So, they gave what they had; and the man was healed.

My dearly beloved, most of the patients that are being led by God through your hands are spiritually blind. They need a Christian nurse/midwife who has something extraordinary that will change their situation for the better. Jesus, the Great Physician, can heal their physical ailments and their spiritual diseases.

Remember you can only give what you have. You cannot give what you don't have. If you have Jesus and His power is in you, give it out. The world is in dire need of a situation changer--our Lord and Master Jesus Christ. Jesus is looking for a willing and an available vessel to reach out to the sick and the needy in the health care institution.

My prayer for you: *May the Almighty God be with you as you avail yourself unto the Lord so He might use you to impact your workplace with the gospel of salvation through your nursing care. Amen.*

Read: Acts 3:1-5

Reflect: Review your previous encounters at work. Was there a time when you could have given Jesus instead of meeting a physical need?

Prayer: Repeat the above prayer

References

1. International Council of Nursing Strategic Priorities: https://www.icn.ch/nursing-policy/icn-strategic-priorities
2. The ICN Code of Ethics for Nurses by International Council of Nurses (ICN) (2012). http://www.old.icn.ch/images/stories/documents/about/icncode_english.pdf
3. NCFI, About NCFI https://ncfi.org/about-ncfi/
4. Integrity, International Standard Bible Encyclopedia (ISBE) by W. L. Walker https://www.internationalstandardbible.com/I/integrity.html
5. Love, International Standard Bible Encyclopedia (ISBE) by William Evans https://www.internationalstandardbible.com/L/love.html
6. Workers in the Vineyard (Matthew 20:1-16) by Allen Ross https://bible.org/seriespage/29-workers-vineyard-matthew-201-16
7. My Heart Christ's Home, by Robert Boyd Munger (1954) https://www.usna.edu/Navigators/_files/documents/MHCH.pdf
8. Brahms Lullaby https://www.youtube.com/watch?v=t894eGoymio
9. H2617 - ḥesed̲ - Strong's Hebrew Lexicon (KJV). Retrieved from https://www.blueletterbible.org//lang/Lexicon/Lexicon.cfm?Strongs=H2617&t=KJV
10. Humility, by Andrew Murray (1884)
11. Go to Dark Gethsemane, by James Montgomery (1825)
12. Grief. Marriam-Webster https://www.merriam-webster.com/dictionary/grief
13. Jehovah's Witnesses https://en.wikipedia.org/wiki/Jehovah%27s_Witnesses
14. Mormons https://en.wikipedia.org/wiki/Mormons
15. IHS Saline Process https://www.ihsglobal.org/SalineProcess
16. Blessing of the Hands Ceremony https://ncf-jcn.org/resources/blessing-hands
17. Save Merriam-Webster https://www.merriam-webster.com/dictionary/save
18. Empathy Merriam-Webster https://www.merriam-webster.com/dictionary/empathy

Author Listing

Tove Giske, Norway,
NCFI President

Carrie M. Dameron, USA
NCFI International Board Member

Martha Fernández Moyano, Argentina
NCFI International Board Member

Steve Fouch, United Kingdom
NCFI International Board Member

Bulbuli Mollick, Bangladesh
NCFI International Board Member

Ishaku Izang. Nigeria
NCFI International Board Member

Gladys Altamirano Garrido, Chile
NCFI International Board Member

Swee Eng Goh, Singapore
Member of NCFI Prayer & Care Committee

About Carrie

Carrie has over 25 years of nursing experience which includes acute care, home care/hospice, gerontology and most recently teaching. She is currently an Associate Professor/Director of a two-year RN program in California, USA. She serves on the International Board for NCFI and the chair of the Prayer and Care Committee since 2016. Carrie is the author/editor for NCFI Cares since its inception in 2013 where she has the honor of encouraging and supporting nurses around the world to live out their love for Jesus in nursing. ncfi.cares@gmail.com

About Martha

Martha is retired from Nursing after 32 years of work, as a Nursing professional and supervisor. She is a member of the International Board Nurses Christian Fellowship International and a member of the Prayer and Care committee. She serves as president of the Christian Union of Argentine Nurses, UCEA.

NCFI & IICN

Through **Nurses Christian Fellowship International (NCFI),** nurses and midwives from all generations, cultures and areas of practice can join together in sharing knowledge, fellowship, friendship and networking through regional conferences, the World Congress, online groups, and courses.

The organisation is comprised of National Nurses Christian Fellowships (NNCFs) from all parts of the world. National NCFs can find inspiration, encouragement and shared resources through NCFI, as can individual nurses who do not have access to a national NCF group. https://ncfi.org/about-ncfi/

Resources:

- CARES: Reflections for Nurses -- compilation of NCFI Cares as free pdf
- NCFI Cares – bimonthly devotions sent via email/Facebook
- Connections Newsletter – stay updated with the latest NCFI news from around the world.
- NCFI Quarterly Prayer Guides – prayer requests/praise reports for NCFI, regions, and member/contact countries.
- https://ncfi.org/resources/general-resources/

International Institute for Christian Nursing (IICN) is committed to the development and offering of various non-academic courses which engage nurses from across the globe in learning more about the integration of a Christian worldview into their nursing practice, education, leadership, and research.

IICN offers nurses Christian perspectives and professional development courses, a free online journal, and a growing collection of resources. https://ncfi.org/about-iicn/

Resources:

- Christian Nurse International (CNI Journal)
- Nursing Focused Bible Studies

Professional Development Courses:

- The Art and Science of Spiritual Care (ASSC)
- Biblical Leadership in Nursing
- Values-Based Teacher

Partnership Courses:

- Saline Process Witness Training
- Faith Community Nursing

https://ncfi.org/resources/iicn-resources/

Get and Stay Connected:
Blog: https://ncfi.org/blog/
Facebook: https://www.facebook.com/visit.ncfi/
Twitter: @ncfinternational
Email: ncfi.cares@ncfi.org

Made in the USA
Monee, IL
26 April 2023

32392230R00046